Reclamation

DAILY JOURNAL

I am saying YES to myself.

_____

Lost and found? Please call

_____

for heaps of good karma.

STRATEJOY

MY THEME FOR THE YEAR

MY 3 BIGGEST GOALS

MY TOP 5 WAYS OF BEING

January

JANUARY

IN DECEMBER, I WAS PROUD OF...

IN DECEMBER, I WAS CHALLENGED BY...

THEME

WAYS OF BEING

THIS MONTH, HONORING MY THEME AND WAYS OF BEING MEANS...

daily prompt

HOW CAN I COMMIT TO MY OWN LIFE TODAY?

Oh yes, this is the reminder that everything starts by showing the fuck up for your life!

January is the perfect time to build momentum by choosing yourself day in and day out.

Choose your goals, choose your commitments to yourself, choose your dreams...

Ownership of your life is *both* the big vision and the small daily tasks. You are the ruler of your world -- so let it be known.

What will your commitment look like today?

DATE:

GRATITUDE	FOCUS
1.	
2.	
3.	

HEADSPACE

HEARTSPACE

TODAY I AM CHOOSING TO BELIEVE...

TODAY I AM HONORING _____ BY:

HOW CAN I COMMIT TO MY OWN LIFE TODAY?

1.

2.

3.

DATE:

GRATITUDE	FOCUS
1.	
2.	
3.	

HEADSPACE

HEARTSPACE

TODAY I AM CHOOSING TO BELIEVE...

TODAY I AM HONORING _____ BY:

HOW CAN I COMMIT TO MY OWN LIFE TODAY?

1.

2.

3.

DATE:

GRATITUDE	FOCUS
1.	
2.	
3.	

HEADSPACE			HEARTSPACE

TODAY I AM CHOOSING TO BELIEVE...

TODAY I AM HONORING _____ BY:

HOW CAN I COMMIT TO MY OWN LIFE TODAY?

1.

2.

3.

DATE:

GRATITUDE	FOCUS
1.	
2.	
3.	

HEADSPACE

HEARTSPACE

TODAY I AM CHOOSING TO BELIEVE...

TODAY I AM HONORING _____ BY:

HOW CAN I COMMIT TO MY OWN LIFE TODAY?

1.

2.

3.

DATE:

GRATITUDE	FOCUS
1.	
2.	
3.	

HEADSPACE

HEARTSPACE

TODAY I AM CHOOSING TO BELIEVE...

TODAY I AM HONORING _____ BY:

HOW CAN I COMMIT TO MY OWN LIFE TODAY?

1.

2.

3.

DATE:

GRATITUDE	FOCUS
1.	
2.	
3.	

HEADSPACE

HEARTSPACE

TODAY I AM CHOOSING TO BELIEVE...

TODAY I AM HONORING _____ BY:

HOW CAN I COMMIT TO MY OWN LIFE TODAY?

1.

2.

3.

DATE:

GRATITUDE	FOCUS
1.	
2.	
3.	

HEADSPACE

HEARTSPACE

TODAY I AM CHOOSING TO BELIEVE...

TODAY I AM HONORING _____ BY:

HOW CAN I COMMIT TO MY OWN LIFE TODAY?

1.

2.

3.

DATE:

GRATITUDE	FOCUS
1.	
2.	
3.	

HEADSPACE | | | **HEARTSPACE**

TODAY I AM CHOOSING TO BELIEVE...

TODAY I AM HONORING _____ BY:

HOW CAN I COMMIT TO MY OWN LIFE TODAY?

1.

2.

3.

DATE:

GRATITUDE	FOCUS
1.	
2.	
3.	

HEADSPACE

HEARTSPACE

TODAY I AM CHOOSING TO BELIEVE...

TODAY I AM HONORING _____ BY:

HOW CAN I COMMIT TO MY OWN LIFE TODAY?

1.

2.

3.

DATE:

GRATITUDE	FOCUS
1.	
2.	
3.	

HEADSPACE

HEARTSPACE

TODAY I AM CHOOSING TO BELIEVE...

TODAY I AM HONORING _____ BY:

HOW CAN I COMMIT TO MY OWN LIFE TODAY?

1.

2.

3.

DATE:

GRATITUDE	FOCUS
1.	
2.	
3.	

HEADSPACE

HEARTSPACE

TODAY I AM CHOOSING TO BELIEVE...

TODAY I AM HONORING _____ BY:

HOW CAN I COMMIT TO MY OWN LIFE TODAY?

1.

2.

3.

DATE:

GRATITUDE	FOCUS
1.	
2.	
3.	

HEADSPACE

HEARTSPACE

TODAY I AM CHOOSING TO BELIEVE...

TODAY I AM HONORING _____ BY:

HOW CAN I COMMIT TO MY OWN LIFE TODAY?

1.

2.

3.

DATE:

GRATITUDE	FOCUS
1.	
2.	
3.	

HEADSPACE

HEARTSPACE

TODAY I AM CHOOSING TO BELIEVE...

TODAY I AM HONORING _____ BY:

HOW CAN I COMMIT TO MY OWN LIFE TODAY?

1.

2.

3.

DATE:

GRATITUDE	FOCUS
1.	
2.	
3.	

HEADSPACE

HEARTSPACE

TODAY I AM CHOOSING TO BELIEVE...

TODAY I AM HONORING _____ BY:

HOW CAN I COMMIT TO MY OWN LIFE TODAY?

1.

2.

3.

DATE:

GRATITUDE	FOCUS
1.	
2.	
3.	

HEADSPACE

HEARTSPACE

TODAY I AM CHOOSING TO BELIEVE...

TODAY I AM HONORING _____ BY:

HOW CAN I COMMIT TO MY OWN LIFE TODAY?

1.

2.

3.

DATE:

GRATITUDE	FOCUS
1.	
2.	
3.	

HEADSPACE

HEARTSPACE

TODAY I AM CHOOSING TO BELIEVE...

TODAY I AM HONORING _____ BY:

HOW CAN I COMMIT TO MY OWN LIFE TODAY?

1.

2.

3.

DATE:

GRATITUDE	FOCUS
1.	
2.	
3.	

HEADSPACE

HEARTSPACE

TODAY I AM CHOOSING TO BELIEVE...

TODAY I AM HONORING _____ BY:

HOW CAN I COMMIT TO MY OWN LIFE TODAY?

1.

2.

3.

DATE:

GRATITUDE	FOCUS
1.	
2.	
3.	

HEADSPACE

HEARTSPACE

TODAY I AM CHOOSING TO BELIEVE...

TODAY I AM HONORING _____ BY:

HOW CAN I COMMIT TO MY OWN LIFE TODAY?

1.

2.

3.

DATE:

GRATITUDE	FOCUS
1.	
2.	
3.	

HEADSPACE

HEARTSPACE

TODAY I AM CHOOSING TO BELIEVE...

TODAY I AM HONORING _____ BY:

HOW CAN I COMMIT TO MY OWN LIFE TODAY?

1.

2.

3.

DATE:

GRATITUDE	FOCUS
1.	
2.	
3.	

HEADSPACE

HEARTSPACE

TODAY I AM CHOOSING TO BELIEVE...

TODAY I AM HONORING _____ BY:

HOW CAN I COMMIT TO MY OWN LIFE TODAY?

1.

2.

3.

February

FEBRUARY

IN JANUARY, I WAS PROUD OF...

IN JANUARY, I WAS CHALLENGED BY...

THEME

WAYS OF BEING

THIS MONTH, HONORING MY THEME AND WAYS OF BEING MEANS...

daily prompt

3 WAYS I CAN BE/WAS TRULY MYSELF?

Whether you are starting or ending your day with this journaling ritual, what does it mean to truly be yourself?

Perhaps it's a certain way of interacting, a quirky dance move, a lunch choice, or speaking your truth. Perhaps it's a boundary drawn, smiling at a stranger, or the really huge hoop earrings.

How can you applaud your own daily choices that reveal more and more of your true self?

How can you challenge yourself to drop another layer of protective mask or please yourself before pleasing another?

DATE:

GRATITUDE	FOCUS
1.	
2.	
3.	

HEADSPACE

HEARTSPACE

TODAY I AM CHOOSING TO BELIEVE...

TODAY I AM HONORING _____ BY:

3 WAYS I CAN BE / WAS TRULY MYSELF:

1.

2.

3.

DATE:

GRATITUDE	FOCUS
1.	
2.	
3.	

HEADSPACE

HEARTSPACE

TODAY I AM CHOOSING TO BELIEVE...

TODAY I AM HONORING _____ BY:

3 WAYS I CAN BE / WAS TRULY MYSELF:

1.

2.

3.

DATE:

GRATITUDE	FOCUS
1.	
2.	
3.	

HEADSPACE			HEARTSPACE

TODAY I AM CHOOSING TO BELIEVE...

TODAY I AM HONORING _____ BY:

3 WAYS I CAN BE / WAS TRULY MYSELF:

1.

2.

3.

DATE:

GRATITUDE	FOCUS
1.	
2.	
3.	

HEADSPACE

HEARTSPACE

TODAY I AM CHOOSING TO BELIEVE...

TODAY I AM HONORING _____ BY:

3 WAYS I CAN BE / WAS TRULY MYSELF:

1.

2.

3.

DATE:

GRATITUDE	FOCUS
1.	
2.	
3.	

HEADSPACE

HEARTSPACE

TODAY I AM CHOOSING TO BELIEVE...

TODAY I AM HONORING _____ BY:

3 WAYS I CAN BE / WAS TRULY MYSELF:

1.

2.

3.

DATE:

GRATITUDE	FOCUS
1.	
2.	
3.	

HEADSPACE | | | HEARTSPACE

TODAY I AM CHOOSING TO BELIEVE...

TODAY I AM HONORING _____ BY:

3 WAYS I CAN BE / WAS TRULY MYSELF:

1.

2.

3.

DATE:

GRATITUDE	FOCUS
1.	
2.	
3.	

HEADSPACE

HEARTSPACE

TODAY I AM CHOOSING TO BELIEVE...

TODAY I AM HONORING _____ BY:

3 WAYS I CAN BE / WAS TRULY MYSELF:

1.

2.

3.

DATE:

GRATITUDE	FOCUS
1.	
2.	
3.	

HEADSPACE

HEARTSPACE

TODAY I AM CHOOSING TO BELIEVE...

TODAY I AM HONORING _____ BY:

3 WAYS I CAN BE / WAS TRULY MYSELF:

1.

2.

3.

DATE:

GRATITUDE	FOCUS
1.	
2.	
3.	

HEADSPACE

HEARTSPACE

TODAY I AM CHOOSING TO BELIEVE...

TODAY I AM HONORING _____ BY:

3 WAYS I CAN BE / WAS TRULY MYSELF:

1.

2.

3.

DATE:

GRATITUDE	FOCUS
1.	
2.	
3.	

HEADSPACE

HEARTSPACE

TODAY I AM CHOOSING TO BELIEVE...

TODAY I AM HONORING _____ BY:

3 WAYS I CAN BE / WAS TRULY MYSELF:

1.

2.

3.

DATE:

GRATITUDE	FOCUS
1.	
2.	
3.	

HEADSPACE

HEARTSPACE

TODAY I AM CHOOSING TO BELIEVE...

TODAY I AM HONORING _____ BY:

3 WAYS I CAN BE / WAS TRULY MYSELF:

1.

2.

3.

DATE:

GRATITUDE	FOCUS
1.	
2.	
3.	

HEADSPACE

HEARTSPACE

TODAY I AM CHOOSING TO BELIEVE...

TODAY I AM HONORING _____ BY:

3 WAYS I CAN BE / WAS TRULY MYSELF:

1.

2.

3.

DATE:

GRATITUDE	FOCUS
1.	
2.	
3.	

HEADSPACE

HEARTSPACE

TODAY I AM CHOOSING TO BELIEVE...

TODAY I AM HONORING _____ BY:

3 WAYS I CAN BE / WAS TRULY MYSELF:

1.

2.

3.

DATE:

GRATITUDE	FOCUS
1.	
2.	
3.	

HEADSPACE

HEARTSPACE

TODAY I AM CHOOSING TO BELIEVE...

TODAY I AM HONORING _____ BY:

3 WAYS I CAN BE / WAS TRULY MYSELF:

1.

2.

3.

DATE:

GRATITUDE	FOCUS
1.	
2.	
3.	

HEADSPACE

HEARTSPACE

TODAY I AM CHOOSING TO BELIEVE...

TODAY I AM HONORING _____ BY:

3 WAYS I CAN BE / WAS TRULY MYSELF:

1.

2.

3.

DATE:

GRATITUDE	FOCUS
1.	
2.	
3.	

HEADSPACE

HEARTSPACE

TODAY I AM CHOOSING TO BELIEVE...

TODAY I AM HONORING _____ BY:

3 WAYS I CAN BE / WAS TRULY MYSELF:

1.

2.

3.

DATE:

GRATITUDE	FOCUS
1.	
2.	
3.	

HEADSPACE

HEARTSPACE

TODAY I AM CHOOSING TO BELIEVE...

TODAY I AM HONORING _____ BY:

3 WAYS I CAN BE / WAS TRULY MYSELF:

1.

2.

3.

DATE:

GRATITUDE	FOCUS
1.	
2.	
3.	

HEADSPACE

HEARTSPACE

TODAY I AM CHOOSING TO BELIEVE...

TODAY I AM HONORING _____ BY:

3 WAYS I CAN BE / WAS TRULY MYSELF:

1.

2.

3.

DATE:

GRATITUDE	FOCUS
1.	
2.	
3.	

HEADSPACE

HEARTSPACE

TODAY I AM CHOOSING TO BELIEVE...

TODAY I AM HONORING _____ BY:

3 WAYS I CAN BE / WAS TRULY MYSELF:

1.

2.

3.

DATE:

GRATITUDE	FOCUS
1.	
2.	
3.	

HEADSPACE

HEARTSPACE

TODAY I AM CHOOSING TO BELIEVE...

TODAY I AM HONORING _____ BY:

3 WAYS I CAN BE / WAS TRULY MYSELF:

1.

2.

3.

March

MARCH

IN FEBRUARY, I WAS PROUD OF...

IN FEBRUARY, I WAS CHALLENGED BY...

THEME

WAYS OF BEING

THIS MONTH, HONORING MY THEME AND WAYS OF BEING MEANS...

daily prompt

I HANDLE ANYTHING THAT LIFE THROWS AT ME. I AM CAPABLE. I DEFY EXPECTATIONS. AND I...

You are creating a daily affirmation chant. Add your own statement to the mix and then read the sentences out loud.

Need some ideas for your own empowering sentence? Here you go!

Swearing and sass totally allowed.

- I am a bad ass bitch.
- I carve my own path.
- I don't need to follow the rules.

DATE:

GRATITUDE	FOCUS
1.	
2.	
3.	

HEADSPACE

HEARTSPACE

TODAY I AM CHOOSING TO BELIEVE...

TODAY I AM HONORING _____ BY:

I HANDLE ANYTHING THAT LIFE THROWS AT ME. I AM CAPABLE. I DEFY EXPECTATIONS. AND I...

1.

2.

3.

DATE:

GRATITUDE	FOCUS
1.	
2.	
3.	

HEADSPACE

HEARTSPACE

TODAY I AM CHOOSING TO BELIEVE...

TODAY I AM HONORING _____ BY:

I HANDLE ANYTHING THAT LIFE THROWS AT ME. I AM CAPABLE. I DEFY EXPECTATIONS. AND I...

1.

2.

3.

DATE:

GRATITUDE	FOCUS
1.	
2.	
3.	

HEADSPACE

HEARTSPACE

TODAY I AM CHOOSING TO BELIEVE...

TODAY I AM HONORING _____ BY:

I HANDLE ANYTHING THAT LIFE THROWS AT ME. I AM CAPABLE. I DEFY EXPECTATIONS. AND I...

1.

2.

3.

DATE:

GRATITUDE	FOCUS
1.	
2.	
3.	

HEADSPACE

HEARTSPACE

TODAY I AM CHOOSING TO BELIEVE...

TODAY I AM HONORING _____ BY:

I HANDLE ANYTHING THAT LIFE THROWS AT ME. I AM CAPABLE. I DEFY EXPECTATIONS. AND I...

1.

2.

3.

DATE:

GRATITUDE	FOCUS
1.	
2.	
3.	

HEADSPACE

HEARTSPACE

TODAY I AM CHOOSING TO BELIEVE...

TODAY I AM HONORING _____ BY:

I HANDLE ANYTHING THAT LIFE THROWS AT ME. I AM CAPABLE. I DEFY EXPECTATIONS. AND I...

1.

2.

3.

DATE:

GRATITUDE	FOCUS
1.	
2.	
3.	

HEADSPACE

HEARTSPACE

TODAY I AM CHOOSING TO BELIEVE...

TODAY I AM HONORING _____ BY:

I HANDLE ANYTHING THAT LIFE THROWS AT ME. I AM CAPABLE. I DEFY EXPECTATIONS. AND I...

1.

2.

3.

DATE:

GRATITUDE	FOCUS
1.	
2.	
3.	

HEADSPACE

HEARTSPACE

TODAY I AM CHOOSING TO BELIEVE...

TODAY I AM HONORING _____ BY:

I HANDLE ANYTHING THAT LIFE THROWS AT ME. I AM CAPABLE.
I DEFY EXPECTATIONS. AND I...

1.

2.

3.

DATE:

GRATITUDE	FOCUS
1.	
2.	
3.	

HEADSPACE

HEARTSPACE

TODAY I AM CHOOSING TO BELIEVE...

TODAY I AM HONORING _____ BY:

I HANDLE ANYTHING THAT LIFE THROWS AT ME. I AM CAPABLE. I DEFY EXPECTATIONS. AND I...

1.

2.

3.

DATE:

GRATITUDE	FOCUS
1.	
2.	
3.	

HEADSPACE

HEARTSPACE

TODAY I AM CHOOSING TO BELIEVE...

TODAY I AM HONORING _____ BY:

I HANDLE ANYTHING THAT LIFE THROWS AT ME. I AM CAPABLE. I DEFY EXPECTATIONS. AND I...

1.

2.

3.

DATE:

GRATITUDE	FOCUS
1.	
2.	
3.	

HEADSPACE

HEARTSPACE

TODAY I AM CHOOSING TO BELIEVE...

TODAY I AM HONORING _____ BY:

I HANDLE ANYTHING THAT LIFE THROWS AT ME. I AM CAPABLE. I DEFY EXPECTATIONS. AND I...

1.

2.

3.

DATE:

GRATITUDE	FOCUS
1.	
2.	
3.	

HEADSPACE

HEARTSPACE

TODAY I AM CHOOSING TO BELIEVE...

TODAY I AM HONORING _____ BY:

I HANDLE ANYTHING THAT LIFE THROWS AT ME. I AM CAPABLE. I DEFY EXPECTATIONS. AND I...

1.

2.

3.

DATE:

GRATITUDE	FOCUS
1.	
2.	
3.	

HEADSPACE			HEARTSPACE

TODAY I AM CHOOSING TO BELIEVE...

TODAY I AM HONORING _____ BY:

I HANDLE ANYTHING THAT LIFE THROWS AT ME. I AM CAPABLE. I DEFY EXPECTATIONS. AND I...

1.

2.

3.

DATE:

GRATITUDE	FOCUS
1.	
2.	
3.	

HEADSPACE

HEARTSPACE

TODAY I AM CHOOSING TO BELIEVE...

TODAY I AM HONORING _____ BY:

I HANDLE ANYTHING THAT LIFE THROWS AT ME. I AM CAPABLE. I DEFY EXPECTATIONS. AND I...

1.

2.

3.

DATE:

GRATITUDE	FOCUS
1.	
2.	
3.	

HEADSPACE

HEARTSPACE

TODAY I AM CHOOSING TO BELIEVE...

TODAY I AM HONORING _____ BY:

I HANDLE ANYTHING THAT LIFE THROWS AT ME. I AM CAPABLE. I DEFY EXPECTATIONS. AND I...

1.

2.

3.

DATE:

GRATITUDE	FOCUS
1.	
2.	
3.	

HEADSPACE

HEARTSPACE

TODAY I AM CHOOSING TO BELIEVE...

TODAY I AM HONORING _____ BY:

I HANDLE ANYTHING THAT LIFE THROWS AT ME. I AM CAPABLE. I DEFY EXPECTATIONS. AND I...

1.

2.

3.

DATE:

GRATITUDE	FOCUS
1.	
2.	
3.	

HEADSPACE   **HEARTSPACE**

TODAY I AM CHOOSING TO BELIEVE...

TODAY I AM HONORING _____ BY:

I HANDLE ANYTHING THAT LIFE THROWS AT ME. I AM CAPABLE. I DEFY EXPECTATIONS. AND I...

1.

2.

3.

DATE:

GRATITUDE	FOCUS
1. 2. 3.	

HEADSPACE			HEARTSPACE

TODAY I AM CHOOSING TO BELIEVE...

TODAY I AM HONORING _____ BY:

I HANDLE ANYTHING THAT LIFE THROWS AT ME. I AM CAPABLE. I DEFY EXPECTATIONS. AND I...

1.

2.

3.

DATE:

GRATITUDE	FOCUS
1.	
2.	
3.	

HEADSPACE

HEARTSPACE

TODAY I AM CHOOSING TO BELIEVE...

TODAY I AM HONORING _____ BY:

I HANDLE ANYTHING THAT LIFE THROWS AT ME. I AM CAPABLE. I DEFY EXPECTATIONS. AND I...

1.

2.

3.

DATE:

GRATITUDE	FOCUS
1.	
2.	
3.	

HEADSPACE

HEARTSPACE

TODAY I AM CHOOSING TO BELIEVE...

TODAY I AM HONORING _____ BY:

I HANDLE ANYTHING THAT LIFE THROWS AT ME. I AM CAPABLE. I DEFY EXPECTATIONS. AND I...

1.

2.

3.

DATE:

GRATITUDE	FOCUS
1.	
2.	
3.	

HEADSPACE

HEARTSPACE

TODAY I AM CHOOSING TO BELIEVE...

TODAY I AM HONORING _____ BY:

I HANDLE ANYTHING THAT LIFE THROWS AT ME. I AM CAPABLE. I DEFY EXPECTATIONS. AND I...

1.

2.

3.

April

APRIL

IN MARCH, I WAS PROUD OF...

IN MARCH, I WAS CHALLENGED BY...

THEME

WAYS OF BEING

THIS MONTH, HONORING MY THEME AND WAYS OF BEING MEANS...

daily prompt

1 THING I LOVE ABOUT MY BODY?
1 THING I RESPECT ABOUT MY BODY?

Write 2 true + positive things about your body.

There's extra magic and bonus points for doing these prompts naked in front of a mirror!

No buts, or feeling critical, or negative self-talk allowed.

It might help to remember the 3 angles of self-compassion while practicing this body love.

- Kindness
- Common Humanity
- Mindfulness

DATE:

GRATITUDE 1. 2. 3.	FOCUS

<table>
<tr><td>HEADSPACE</td><td></td><td></td><td>HEARTSPACE</td></tr>
</table>

TODAY I AM CHOOSING TO BELIEVE...

TODAY I AM HONORING _____ BY:

1 THING I LOVE ABOUT MY BODY?

1 THING I RESPECT ABOUT MY BODY?

DATE:

GRATITUDE	FOCUS
1.	
2.	
3.	

HEADSPACE

HEARTSPACE

TODAY I AM CHOOSING TO BELIEVE...

TODAY I AM HONORING _____ BY:

1 THING I LOVE ABOUT MY BODY?

1 THING I RESPECT ABOUT MY BODY?

DATE:

GRATITUDE	FOCUS
1.	
2.	
3.	

HEADSPACE

HEARTSPACE

TODAY I AM CHOOSING TO BELIEVE...

TODAY I AM HONORING _____ BY:

1 THING I LOVE ABOUT MY BODY?

1 THING I RESPECT ABOUT MY BODY?

DATE:

GRATITUDE	FOCUS
1.	
2.	
3.	

HEADSPACE

HEARTSPACE

TODAY I AM CHOOSING TO BELIEVE...

TODAY I AM HONORING _____ BY:

1 THING I LOVE ABOUT MY BODY?

1 THING I RESPECT ABOUT MY BODY?

DATE:

GRATITUDE	FOCUS
1.	
2.	
3.	

HEADSPACE			HEARTSPACE

TODAY I AM CHOOSING TO BELIEVE...

TODAY I AM HONORING _____ BY:

1 THING I LOVE ABOUT MY BODY?

1 THING I RESPECT ABOUT MY BODY?

DATE:

GRATITUDE	FOCUS
1.	
2.	
3.	

HEADSPACE | | | **HEARTSPACE**

TODAY I AM CHOOSING TO BELIEVE...

TODAY I AM HONORING _____ BY:

1 THING I LOVE ABOUT MY BODY?

1 THING I RESPECT ABOUT MY BODY?

DATE:

GRATITUDE	FOCUS
1.	
2.	
3.	

HEADSPACE

HEARTSPACE

TODAY I AM CHOOSING TO BELIEVE...

TODAY I AM HONORING _____ BY:

1 THING I LOVE ABOUT MY BODY?

1 THING I RESPECT ABOUT MY BODY?

DATE:

GRATITUDE	FOCUS
1.	
2.	
3.	

HEADSPACE

HEARTSPACE

TODAY I AM CHOOSING TO BELIEVE...

TODAY I AM HONORING _____ BY:

1 THING I LOVE ABOUT MY BODY?

1 THING I RESPECT ABOUT MY BODY?

DATE:

GRATITUDE	FOCUS
1.	
2.	
3.	

HEADSPACE

HEARTSPACE

TODAY I AM CHOOSING TO BELIEVE...

TODAY I AM HONORING _____ BY:

1 THING I LOVE ABOUT MY BODY?

1 THING I RESPECT ABOUT MY BODY?

DATE:

GRATITUDE	FOCUS
1.	
2.	
3.	

HEADSPACE			HEARTSPACE

TODAY I AM CHOOSING TO BELIEVE...

TODAY I AM HONORING _____ BY:

1 THING I LOVE ABOUT MY BODY?

1 THING I RESPECT ABOUT MY BODY?

DATE:

GRATITUDE	FOCUS
1.	
2.	
3.	

HEADSPACE

HEARTSPACE

TODAY I AM CHOOSING TO BELIEVE...

TODAY I AM HONORING _____ BY:

1 THING I LOVE ABOUT MY BODY?

1 THING I RESPECT ABOUT MY BODY?

DATE:

GRATITUDE	FOCUS
1.	
2.	
3.	

HEADSPACE

HEARTSPACE

TODAY I AM CHOOSING TO BELIEVE...

TODAY I AM HONORING _____ BY:

1 THING I LOVE ABOUT MY BODY?

1 THING I RESPECT ABOUT MY BODY?

DATE:

GRATITUDE	FOCUS
1.	
2.	
3.	

HEADSPACE

HEARTSPACE

TODAY I AM CHOOSING TO BELIEVE...

TODAY I AM HONORING _____ BY:

1 THING I LOVE ABOUT MY BODY?

1 THING I RESPECT ABOUT MY BODY?

DATE:

GRATITUDE	FOCUS
1.	
2.	
3.	

HEADSPACE

HEARTSPACE

TODAY I AM CHOOSING TO BELIEVE...

TODAY I AM HONORING _____ BY:

1 THING I LOVE ABOUT MY BODY?

1 THING I RESPECT ABOUT MY BODY?

DATE:

GRATITUDE	FOCUS
1.	
2.	
3.	

HEADSPACE

HEARTSPACE

TODAY I AM CHOOSING TO BELIEVE...

TODAY I AM HONORING _____ BY:

1 THING I LOVE ABOUT MY BODY?

1 THING I RESPECT ABOUT MY BODY?

DATE:

GRATITUDE	FOCUS
1.	
2.	
3.	

HEADSPACE

HEARTSPACE

TODAY I AM CHOOSING TO BELIEVE...

TODAY I AM HONORING _____ BY:

1 THING I LOVE ABOUT MY BODY?

1 THING I RESPECT ABOUT MY BODY?

DATE:

GRATITUDE	FOCUS
1.	
2.	
3.	

HEADSPACE

HEARTSPACE

TODAY I AM CHOOSING TO BELIEVE...

TODAY I AM HONORING _____ BY:

1 THING I LOVE ABOUT MY BODY?

1 THING I RESPECT ABOUT MY BODY?

DATE:

GRATITUDE	FOCUS
1.	
2.	
3.	

HEADSPACE

HEARTSPACE

TODAY I AM CHOOSING TO BELIEVE...

TODAY I AM HONORING _____ BY:

1 THING I LOVE ABOUT MY BODY?

1 THING I RESPECT ABOUT MY BODY?

DATE:

GRATITUDE	FOCUS
1.	
2.	
3.	

HEADSPACE

HEARTSPACE

TODAY I AM CHOOSING TO BELIEVE...

TODAY I AM HONORING _____ BY:

1 THING I LOVE ABOUT MY BODY?

1 THING I RESPECT ABOUT MY BODY?

DATE:

GRATITUDE	FOCUS
1.	
2.	
3.	

HEADSPACE | | | **HEARTSPACE**

TODAY I AM CHOOSING TO BELIEVE...

TODAY I AM HONORING _____ BY:

1 THING I LOVE ABOUT MY BODY?

1 THING I RESPECT ABOUT MY BODY?

May

MAY

IN APRIL, I WAS PROUD OF...

IN APRIL, I WAS CHALLENGED BY...

THEME

WAYS OF BEING

THIS MONTH, HONORING MY THEME AND WAYS OF BEING MEANS...

daily prompt

WHAT IS A SENSUAL PLEASURE I CAN/I DID EXPERIENCE?

This daily ritual is asking you to pay attention to your senses, getting out of your head and into your body.

The point? To train yourself to slow down and celebrate the sensual delights in your world on a more regular basis.

Ask —
What scent gave me pleasure today?
What taste gave me pleasure today?
What sound gave me pleasure today?
What feeling/touch gave me pleasure today?
What sight gave me pleasure today?

As you notice patterns emerging in your pleasure triggers, see if you can plan them into your days!

DATE:

GRATITUDE	FOCUS
1.	
2.	
3.	

HEADSPACE

HEARTSPACE

TODAY I AM CHOOSING TO BELIEVE...

TODAY I AM HONORING _____ BY:

WHAT IS A SENSUAL PLEASURE I CAN/I DID EXPERIENCE?

DATE:

GRATITUDE	FOCUS
1.	
2.	
3.	

HEADSPACE | | | **HEARTSPACE**

TODAY I AM CHOOSING TO BELIEVE...

TODAY I AM HONORING _____ BY:

WHAT IS A SENSUAL PLEASURE I CAN/I DID EXPERIENCE?

DATE:

GRATITUDE	FOCUS
1.	
2.	
3.	

HEADSPACE

HEARTSPACE

TODAY I AM CHOOSING TO BELIEVE...

TODAY I AM HONORING _____ BY:

WHAT IS A SENSUAL PLEASURE I CAN/I DID EXPERIENCE?

DATE:

GRATITUDE	FOCUS
1.	
2.	
3.	

HEADSPACE

HEARTSPACE

TODAY I AM CHOOSING TO BELIEVE...

TODAY I AM HONORING _____ BY:

WHAT IS A SENSUAL PLEASURE I CAN/I DID EXPERIENCE?

DATE:

GRATITUDE	FOCUS
1.	
2.	
3.	

HEADSPACE

HEARTSPACE

TODAY I AM CHOOSING TO BELIEVE...

TODAY I AM HONORING _____ BY:

WHAT IS A SENSUAL PLEASURE I CAN/I DID EXPERIENCE?

DATE:

GRATITUDE	FOCUS
1.	
2.	
3.	

HEADSPACE

HEARTSPACE

TODAY I AM CHOOSING TO BELIEVE...

TODAY I AM HONORING _____ BY:

WHAT IS A SENSUAL PLEASURE I CAN/I DID EXPERIENCE?

DATE:

GRATITUDE	FOCUS
1.	
2.	
3.	

HEADSPACE

HEARTSPACE

TODAY I AM CHOOSING TO BELIEVE...

TODAY I AM HONORING _____ BY:

WHAT IS A SENSUAL PLEASURE I CAN/I DID EXPERIENCE?

DATE:

GRATITUDE	FOCUS
1.	
2.	
3.	

HEADSPACE

HEARTSPACE

TODAY I AM CHOOSING TO BELIEVE...

TODAY I AM HONORING _____ BY:

WHAT IS A SENSUAL PLEASURE I CAN/I DID EXPERIENCE?

DATE:

GRATITUDE	FOCUS
1.	
2.	
3.	

HEADSPACE

HEARTSPACE

TODAY I AM CHOOSING TO BELIEVE...

TODAY I AM HONORING _____ BY:

WHAT IS A SENSUAL PLEASURE I CAN/I DID EXPERIENCE?

DATE:

GRATITUDE	FOCUS
1.	
2.	
3.	

HEADSPACE

HEARTSPACE

TODAY I AM CHOOSING TO BELIEVE...

TODAY I AM HONORING _____ BY:

WHAT IS A SENSUAL PLEASURE I CAN/I DID EXPERIENCE?

DATE:

GRATITUDE	FOCUS
1.	
2.	
3.	

HEADSPACE

HEARTSPACE

TODAY I AM CHOOSING TO BELIEVE...

TODAY I AM HONORING _____ BY:

WHAT IS A SENSUAL PLEASURE I CAN/I DID EXPERIENCE?

DATE:

GRATITUDE	FOCUS
1.	
2.	
3.	

HEADSPACE

HEARTSPACE

TODAY I AM CHOOSING TO BELIEVE...

TODAY I AM HONORING _____ BY:

WHAT IS A SENSUAL PLEASURE I CAN/I DID EXPERIENCE?

DATE:

GRATITUDE	FOCUS
1.	
2.	
3.	

HEADSPACE

HEARTSPACE

TODAY I AM CHOOSING TO BELIEVE...

TODAY I AM HONORING _____ BY:

WHAT IS A SENSUAL PLEASURE I CAN/I DID EXPERIENCE?

DATE:

GRATITUDE	FOCUS
1.	
2.	
3.	

HEADSPACE

HEARTSPACE

TODAY I AM CHOOSING TO BELIEVE...

TODAY I AM HONORING _____ BY:

WHAT IS A SENSUAL PLEASURE I CAN/I DID EXPERIENCE?

DATE:

GRATITUDE	FOCUS
1.	
2.	
3.	

HEADSPACE

HEARTSPACE

TODAY I AM CHOOSING TO BELIEVE...

TODAY I AM HONORING _____ BY:

WHAT IS A SENSUAL PLEASURE I CAN/I DID EXPERIENCE?

DATE:

GRATITUDE	FOCUS
1.	
2.	
3.	

HEADSPACE

HEARTSPACE

TODAY I AM CHOOSING TO BELIEVE...

TODAY I AM HONORING _____ BY:

WHAT IS A SENSUAL PLEASURE I CAN/I DID EXPERIENCE?

DATE:

GRATITUDE	FOCUS
1.	
2.	
3.	

HEADSPACE

HEARTSPACE

TODAY I AM CHOOSING TO BELIEVE...

TODAY I AM HONORING _____ BY:

WHAT IS A SENSUAL PLEASURE I CAN/I DID EXPERIENCE?

DATE:

GRATITUDE	FOCUS
1.	
2.	
3.	

HEADSPACE

HEARTSPACE

TODAY I AM CHOOSING TO BELIEVE...

TODAY I AM HONORING _____ BY:

WHAT IS A SENSUAL PLEASURE I CAN/I DID EXPERIENCE?

DATE:

GRATITUDE	FOCUS
1.	
2.	
3.	

HEADSPACE

HEARTSPACE

TODAY I AM CHOOSING TO BELIEVE...

TODAY I AM HONORING _____ BY:

WHAT IS A SENSUAL PLEASURE I CAN/I DID EXPERIENCE?

DATE:

GRATITUDE	FOCUS
1.	
2.	
3.	

HEADSPACE

HEARTSPACE

TODAY I AM CHOOSING TO BELIEVE...

TODAY I AM HONORING _____ BY:

WHAT IS A SENSUAL PLEASURE I CAN/I DID EXPERIENCE?

June

JUNE

IN MAY, I WAS PROUD OF...

IN MAY, I WAS CHALLENGED BY...

THEME

WAYS OF BEING

THIS MONTH, HONORING MY THEME AND WAYS OF BEING MEANS...

daily prompt

4 OFFERS OF LOVING-KINDNESS?
MAY I... MAY YOU... MAY YOU... MAY WE...

Practice a tiny version of a Metta meditation. Write a wish for humanity and offer it to yourself, a loved one, a stranger, and the entire world. Repeat as needed.

Need an example? Here you go!

May I find peace in my heart.
May you (loved one) find peace in your heart.
May you (stranger) find peace in your heart.
May we find peace in our hearts.

DATE:

GRATITUDE	FOCUS
1.	
2.	
3.	

HEADSPACE

HEARTSPACE

TODAY I AM CHOOSING TO BELIEVE...

TODAY I AM HONORING _____ BY:

4 OFFERS OF LOVING-KINDNESS? MAY I... MAY YOU... MAY YOU... MAY WE...

1.

2.

3.

4.

DATE:

GRATITUDE	FOCUS
1.	
2.	
3.	

HEADSPACE

HEARTSPACE

TODAY I AM CHOOSING TO BELIEVE...

TODAY I AM HONORING _____ BY:

4 OFFERS OF LOVING-KINDNESS? MAY I... MAY YOU... MAY YOU... MAY WE...

1.

2.

3.

4.

DATE:

GRATITUDE	FOCUS
1.	
2.	
3.	

HEADSPACE

HEARTSPACE

TODAY I AM CHOOSING TO BELIEVE...

TODAY I AM HONORING _____ BY:

4 OFFERS OF LOVING-KINDNESS? MAY I... MAY YOU... MAY YOU... MAY WE...

1.

2.

3.

4.

DATE:

GRATITUDE	FOCUS
1.	
2.	
3.	

HEADSPACE | | | HEARTSPACE

TODAY I AM CHOOSING TO BELIEVE...

TODAY I AM HONORING _____ BY:

4 OFFERS OF LOVING-KINDNESS? MAY I... MAY YOU... MAY YOU... MAY WE...

1.

2.

3.

4.

DATE:

GRATITUDE	FOCUS
1.	
2.	
3.	

HEADSPACE

HEARTSPACE

TODAY I AM CHOOSING TO BELIEVE...

TODAY I AM HONORING _____ BY:

4 OFFERS OF LOVING-KINDNESS? MAY I... MAY YOU... MAY YOU... MAY WE...

1.

2.

3.

4.

DATE:

GRATITUDE	FOCUS
1.	
2.	
3.	

HEADSPACE

HEARTSPACE

TODAY I AM CHOOSING TO BELIEVE...

TODAY I AM HONORING _____ BY:

4 OFFERS OF LOVING-KINDNESS? MAY I... MAY YOU... MAY YOU... MAY WE...

1.

2.

3.

4.

DATE:

GRATITUDE	FOCUS
1.	
2.	
3.	

HEADSPACE

HEARTSPACE

TODAY I AM CHOOSING TO BELIEVE...

TODAY I AM HONORING _____ BY:

4 OFFERS OF LOVING-KINDNESS? MAY I... MAY YOU... MAY YOU... MAY WE...

1.

2.

3.

4.

DATE:

GRATITUDE	FOCUS
1.	
2.	
3.	

HEADSPACE			HEARTSPACE

TODAY I AM CHOOSING TO BELIEVE...

TODAY I AM HONORING _____ BY:

4 OFFERS OF LOVING-KINDNESS? MAY I... MAY YOU... MAY YOU... MAY WE...

1.

2.

3.

4.

DATE:

GRATITUDE	FOCUS
1.	
2.	
3.	

HEADSPACE

HEARTSPACE

TODAY I AM CHOOSING TO BELIEVE...

TODAY I AM HONORING _____ BY:

4 OFFERS OF LOVING-KINDNESS? MAY I... MAY YOU... MAY YOU... MAY WE...

1.

2.

3.

4.

DATE:

GRATITUDE	FOCUS
1.	
2.	
3.	

HEADSPACE

HEARTSPACE

TODAY I AM CHOOSING TO BELIEVE...

TODAY I AM HONORING _____ BY:

4 OFFERS OF LOVING-KINDNESS? MAY I... MAY YOU... MAY YOU... MAY WE...

1.

2.

3.

4.

DATE:

GRATITUDE	FOCUS
1.	
2.	
3.	

HEADSPACE

HEARTSPACE

TODAY I AM CHOOSING TO BELIEVE...

TODAY I AM HONORING _____ BY:

4 OFFERS OF LOVING-KINDNESS? MAY I... MAY YOU... MAY YOU... MAY WE...

1.

2.

3.

4.

DATE:

GRATITUDE	FOCUS
1.	
2.	
3.	

HEADSPACE | | | **HEARTSPACE**

TODAY I AM CHOOSING TO BELIEVE...

TODAY I AM HONORING _____ BY:

4 OFFERS OF LOVING-KINDNESS? MAY I... MAY YOU... MAY YOU... MAY WE...

1.

2.

3.

4.

DATE:

GRATITUDE	FOCUS
1.	
2.	
3.	

HEADSPACE			HEARTSPACE

TODAY I AM CHOOSING TO BELIEVE...

TODAY I AM HONORING _____ BY:

4 OFFERS OF LOVING-KINDNESS? MAY I... MAY YOU... MAY YOU... MAY WE...

1.

2.

3.

4.

DATE:

GRATITUDE	FOCUS
1.	
2.	
3.	

HEADSPACE

HEARTSPACE

TODAY I AM CHOOSING TO BELIEVE...

TODAY I AM HONORING _____ BY:

4 OFFERS OF LOVING-KINDNESS? MAY I... MAY YOU... MAY YOU... MAY WE...

1.

2.

3.

4.

DATE:

GRATITUDE	FOCUS
1.	
2.	
3.	

HEADSPACE | | **HEARTSPACE**

TODAY I AM CHOOSING TO BELIEVE...

TODAY I AM HONORING _____ BY:

4 OFFERS OF LOVING-KINDNESS? MAY I... MAY YOU... MAY YOU... MAY WE...

1.

2.

3.

4.

DATE:

GRATITUDE	FOCUS
1.	
2.	
3.	

HEADSPACE

HEARTSPACE

TODAY I AM CHOOSING TO BELIEVE...

TODAY I AM HONORING _____ BY:

4 OFFERS OF LOVING-KINDNESS? MAY I... MAY YOU... MAY YOU... MAY WE...

1.

2.

3.

4.

DATE:

GRATITUDE	FOCUS
1.	
2.	
3.	

HEADSPACE

HEARTSPACE

TODAY I AM CHOOSING TO BELIEVE...

TODAY I AM HONORING _____ BY:

4 OFFERS OF LOVING-KINDNESS? MAY I... MAY YOU... MAY YOU... MAY WE...

1.

2.

3.

4.

DATE:

GRATITUDE	FOCUS
1.	
2.	
3.	

HEADSPACE

HEARTSPACE

TODAY I AM CHOOSING TO BELIEVE...

TODAY I AM HONORING _____ BY:

4 OFFERS OF LOVING-KINDNESS? MAY I... MAY YOU... MAY YOU... MAY WE...

1.

2.

3.

4.

DATE:

GRATITUDE	FOCUS
1.	
2.	
3.	

HEADSPACE

HEARTSPACE

TODAY I AM CHOOSING TO BELIEVE...

TODAY I AM HONORING _____ BY:

4 OFFERS OF LOVING-KINDNESS? MAY I... MAY YOU... MAY YOU... MAY WE...

1.

2.

3.

4.

DATE:

GRATITUDE	FOCUS
1.	
2.	
3.	

HEADSPACE

HEARTSPACE

TODAY I AM CHOOSING TO BELIEVE...

TODAY I AM HONORING _____ BY:

4 OFFERS OF LOVING-KINDNESS? MAY I... MAY YOU... MAY YOU... MAY WE...

1.

2.

3.

4.

July

JULY

IN JUNE, I WAS PROUD OF...

IN JUNE, I WAS CHALLENGED BY...

THEME

WAYS OF BEING

THIS MONTH, HONORING MY THEME AND WAYS OF BEING MEANS...

daily prompt

**I AM CURIOUS ABOUT... I AM INSPIRED BY...
MY BILLBOARD FOR TODAY IS...**

Wonder and awe are avenues to your own creative self-expression. Practice tuning into the ideas, things, places, and people that intrigue and inspire you!

And your billboard is your daily chance to declare something important.

I am Enough.
I can take my dreams seriously, without taking myself seriously.
I practice Joy in a Messy World.

When time allows, take your daily billboard and turn it into a work of art — an instagram quote, a poem, a tiny painting, a love note for your partner, a FB live video, a meal, a personal essay, etc.

DATE:

GRATITUDE	FOCUS
1.	
2.	
3.	

HEADSPACE | | | **HEARTSPACE**

TODAY I AM CHOOSING TO BELIEVE...

TODAY I AM HONORING _____ BY:

I AM CURIOUS ABOUT...	I AM INSPIRED BY...	MY BILLBOARD FOR TODAY IS...

DATE:

GRATITUDE	FOCUS
1.	
2.	
3.	

HEADSPACE | | | **HEARTSPACE**

TODAY I AM CHOOSING TO BELIEVE...

TODAY I AM HONORING _____ BY:

I AM CURIOUS ABOUT...	I AM INSPIRED BY...	MY BILLBOARD FOR TODAY IS...

DATE:

GRATITUDE	FOCUS
1.	
2.	
3.	

HEADSPACE

HEARTSPACE

TODAY I AM CHOOSING TO BELIEVE...

TODAY I AM HONORING _____ BY:

I AM CURIOUS ABOUT...	I AM INSPIRED BY...	MY BILLBOARD FOR TODAY IS...

DATE:

GRATITUDE	FOCUS
1.	
2.	
3.	

HEADSPACE		HEARTSPACE

TODAY I AM CHOOSING TO BELIEVE...

TODAY I AM HONORING _____ BY:

I AM CURIOUS ABOUT...	I AM INSPIRED BY...	MY BILLBOARD FOR TODAY IS...

DATE:

GRATITUDE	FOCUS
1.	
2.	
3.	

HEADSPACE

HEARTSPACE

TODAY I AM CHOOSING TO BELIEVE...

TODAY I AM HONORING _____ BY:

I AM CURIOUS ABOUT...	I AM INSPIRED BY...	MY BILLBOARD FOR TODAY IS...

DATE:

GRATITUDE	FOCUS
1.	
2.	
3.	

HEADSPACE			HEARTSPACE

TODAY I AM CHOOSING TO BELIEVE...

TODAY I AM HONORING _____ BY:

I AM CURIOUS ABOUT...	I AM INSPIRED BY...	MY BILLBOARD FOR TODAY IS...

DATE:

GRATITUDE	FOCUS
1.	
2.	
3.	

HEADSPACE

HEARTSPACE

TODAY I AM CHOOSING TO BELIEVE...

TODAY I AM HONORING _____ BY:

I AM CURIOUS ABOUT...	I AM INSPIRED BY...	MY BILLBOARD FOR TODAY IS...

DATE:

GRATITUDE	FOCUS
1.	
2.	
3.	

HEADSPACE

HEARTSPACE

TODAY I AM CHOOSING TO BELIEVE...

TODAY I AM HONORING _____ BY:

I AM CURIOUS ABOUT...	I AM INSPIRED BY...	MY BILLBOARD FOR TODAY IS...

DATE:

GRATITUDE	FOCUS
1.	
2.	
3.	

HEADSPACE			HEARTSPACE

TODAY I AM CHOOSING TO BELIEVE...

TODAY I AM HONORING _____ BY:

I AM CURIOUS ABOUT...	I AM INSPIRED BY...	MY BILLBOARD FOR TODAY IS...

DATE:

GRATITUDE	FOCUS
1.	
2.	
3.	

HEADSPACE

HEARTSPACE

TODAY I AM CHOOSING TO BELIEVE...

TODAY I AM HONORING _____ BY:

I AM CURIOUS ABOUT...	I AM INSPIRED BY...	MY BILLBOARD FOR TODAY IS...

DATE:

GRATITUDE	FOCUS
1.	
2.	
3.	

HEADSPACE			HEARTSPACE

TODAY I AM CHOOSING TO BELIEVE...

TODAY I AM HONORING _____ BY:

I AM CURIOUS ABOUT...	I AM INSPIRED BY...	MY BILLBOARD FOR TODAY IS...

DATE:

GRATITUDE	FOCUS
1.	
2.	
3.	

HEADSPACE

HEARTSPACE

TODAY I AM CHOOSING TO BELIEVE...

TODAY I AM HONORING _____ BY:

I AM CURIOUS ABOUT...	I AM INSPIRED BY...	MY BILLBOARD FOR TODAY IS...

DATE:

GRATITUDE	FOCUS
1.	
2.	
3.	

HEADSPACE			HEARTSPACE

TODAY I AM CHOOSING TO BELIEVE...

TODAY I AM HONORING _____ BY:

I AM CURIOUS ABOUT...	I AM INSPIRED BY...	MY BILLBOARD FOR TODAY IS...

DATE:

GRATITUDE	FOCUS
1.	
2.	
3.	

HEADSPACE			HEARTSPACE

TODAY I AM CHOOSING TO BELIEVE...

TODAY I AM HONORING _____ BY:

I AM CURIOUS ABOUT...	I AM INSPIRED BY...	MY BILLBOARD FOR TODAY IS...

DATE:

GRATITUDE	FOCUS
1.	
2.	
3.	

HEADSPACE

HEARTSPACE

TODAY I AM CHOOSING TO BELIEVE...

TODAY I AM HONORING _____ BY:

I AM CURIOUS ABOUT...	I AM INSPIRED BY...	MY BILLBOARD FOR TODAY IS...

DATE:

GRATITUDE	FOCUS
1.	
2.	
3.	

HEADSPACE

HEARTSPACE

TODAY I AM CHOOSING TO BELIEVE...

TODAY I AM HONORING _____ BY:

I AM CURIOUS ABOUT...	I AM INSPIRED BY...	MY BILLBOARD FOR TODAY IS...

DATE:

GRATITUDE	FOCUS
1.	
2.	
3.	

HEADSPACE

HEARTSPACE

TODAY I AM CHOOSING TO BELIEVE...

TODAY I AM HONORING _____ BY:

I AM CURIOUS ABOUT...	I AM INSPIRED BY...	MY BILLBOARD FOR TODAY IS...

DATE:

GRATITUDE	FOCUS
1.	
2.	
3.	

HEADSPACE			HEARTSPACE

TODAY I AM CHOOSING TO BELIEVE...

TODAY I AM HONORING _____ BY:

I AM CURIOUS ABOUT...	I AM INSPIRED BY...	MY BILLBOARD FOR TODAY IS...

DATE:

GRATITUDE	FOCUS
1.	
2.	
3.	

HEADSPACE			HEARTSPACE

TODAY I AM CHOOSING TO BELIEVE...

TODAY I AM HONORING _____ BY:

I AM CURIOUS ABOUT...	I AM INSPIRED BY...	MY BILLBOARD FOR TODAY IS...

DATE:

GRATITUDE	FOCUS
1.	
2.	
3.	

HEADSPACE

HEARTSPACE

TODAY I AM CHOOSING TO BELIEVE...

TODAY I AM HONORING _____ BY:

I AM CURIOUS ABOUT...	I AM INSPIRED BY...	MY BILLBOARD FOR TODAY IS...

August

AUGUST

IN JULY, I WAS PROUD OF...

IN JULY, I WAS CHALLENGED BY...

THEME

WAYS OF BEING

THIS MONTH, HONORING MY THEME AND WAYS OF BEING MEANS...

daily prompt

I AM SCARED OF … BUT I'M GOING TO DO THIS…

When you allow yourself to feel fear or anxiety or nerves, but you take action anyway?

That's the definition of courage.

In this prompt, practice naming something that you're scared of and then naming what you're going to do in face of that fear.

I am scared of what "everyone thinks" but I'm going to publish my blog post on being child-free by choice today.

I am scared of "rejection by my partner" but I'm going to wear my silky pajamas tonight instead of my sweats and ask them to come to bed early for sexy time.

I am scared of "looking like an idiot" but I'm going to speak up in the staff meeting today because I think we're getting off track with the marketing campaign.

DATE:

GRATITUDE	FOCUS
1.	
2.	
3.	

HEADSPACE

HEARTSPACE

TODAY I AM CHOOSING TO BELIEVE...

TODAY I AM HONORING _____ BY:

I AM SCARED OF _____
BUT I AM GOING TO DO THIS....

DATE:

GRATITUDE	FOCUS
1.	
2.	
3.	

HEADSPACE

HEARTSPACE

TODAY I AM CHOOSING TO BELIEVE...

TODAY I AM HONORING _____ BY:

I AM SCARED OF _____
BUT I AM GOING TO DO THIS....

DATE:

GRATITUDE	FOCUS
1.	
2.	
3.	

HEADSPACE

HEARTSPACE

TODAY I AM CHOOSING TO BELIEVE...

TODAY I AM HONORING _____ BY:

I AM SCARED OF _____
BUT I AM GOING TO DO THIS....

DATE:

GRATITUDE	FOCUS
1.	
2.	
3.	

HEADSPACE

HEARTSPACE

TODAY I AM CHOOSING TO BELIEVE...

TODAY I AM HONORING _____ BY:

I AM SCARED OF _____

BUT I AM GOING TO DO THIS....

DATE:

GRATITUDE	FOCUS
1.	
2.	
3.	

HEADSPACE			HEARTSPACE

TODAY I AM CHOOSING TO BELIEVE...

TODAY I AM HONORING _____ BY:

I AM SCARED OF _____
BUT I AM GOING TO DO THIS....

DATE:

GRATITUDE	FOCUS
1.	
2.	
3.	

HEADSPACE

HEARTSPACE

TODAY I AM CHOOSING TO BELIEVE...

TODAY I AM HONORING _____ BY:

I AM SCARED OF _____
BUT I AM GOING TO DO THIS....

DATE:

GRATITUDE	FOCUS
1.	
2.	
3.	

HEADSPACE

HEARTSPACE

TODAY I AM CHOOSING TO BELIEVE...

TODAY I AM HONORING _____ BY:

I AM SCARED OF _____
BUT I AM GOING TO DO THIS....

DATE:

GRATITUDE	FOCUS
1.	
2.	
3.	

HEADSPACE | | | **HEARTSPACE**

TODAY I AM CHOOSING TO BELIEVE...

TODAY I AM HONORING _____ BY:

I AM SCARED OF _____
BUT I AM GOING TO DO THIS....

DATE:

GRATITUDE	FOCUS
1.	
2.	
3.	

HEADSPACE			HEARTSPACE

TODAY I AM CHOOSING TO BELIEVE...

TODAY I AM HONORING _____ BY:

I AM SCARED OF _____
BUT I AM GOING TO DO THIS....

DATE:

GRATITUDE	FOCUS
1.	
2.	
3.	

HEADSPACE

HEARTSPACE

TODAY I AM CHOOSING TO BELIEVE...

TODAY I AM HONORING _____ BY:

I AM SCARED OF _____

BUT I AM GOING TO DO THIS....

DATE:

GRATITUDE	FOCUS
1.	
2.	
3.	

HEADSPACE

HEARTSPACE

TODAY I AM CHOOSING TO BELIEVE...

TODAY I AM HONORING _____ BY:

I AM SCARED OF _____
BUT I AM GOING TO DO THIS....

DATE:

GRATITUDE	FOCUS
1.	
2.	
3.	

HEADSPACE

HEARTSPACE

TODAY I AM CHOOSING TO BELIEVE...

TODAY I AM HONORING _____ BY:

I AM SCARED OF _____
BUT I AM GOING TO DO THIS....

DATE:

GRATITUDE	FOCUS
1.	
2.	
3.	

HEADSPACE

HEARTSPACE

TODAY I AM CHOOSING TO BELIEVE...

TODAY I AM HONORING _____ BY:

I AM SCARED OF _____

BUT I AM GOING TO DO THIS....

DATE:

GRATITUDE	FOCUS
1.	
2.	
3.	

HEADSPACE

HEARTSPACE

TODAY I AM CHOOSING TO BELIEVE...

TODAY I AM HONORING _____ BY:

I AM SCARED OF _____
BUT I AM GOING TO DO THIS....

DATE:

GRATITUDE	FOCUS
1.	
2.	
3.	

HEADSPACE

HEARTSPACE

TODAY I AM CHOOSING TO BELIEVE...

TODAY I AM HONORING _____ BY:

I AM SCARED OF _____
BUT I AM GOING TO DO THIS....

DATE:

GRATITUDE	FOCUS
1.	
2.	
3.	

HEADSPACE

HEARTSPACE

TODAY I AM CHOOSING TO BELIEVE...

TODAY I AM HONORING _____ BY:

I AM SCARED OF _____
BUT I AM GOING TO DO THIS....

DATE:

GRATITUDE	FOCUS
1.	
2.	
3.	

HEADSPACE

HEARTSPACE

TODAY I AM CHOOSING TO BELIEVE...

TODAY I AM HONORING _____ BY:

I AM SCARED OF _____

BUT I AM GOING TO DO THIS....

DATE:

GRATITUDE	FOCUS
1.	
2.	
3.	

HEADSPACE

HEARTSPACE

TODAY I AM CHOOSING TO BELIEVE...

TODAY I AM HONORING _____ BY:

I AM SCARED OF _____
BUT I AM GOING TO DO THIS....

DATE:

GRATITUDE	FOCUS
1.	
2.	
3.	

HEADSPACE

HEARTSPACE

TODAY I AM CHOOSING TO BELIEVE...

TODAY I AM HONORING _____ BY:

I AM SCARED OF _____
BUT I AM GOING TO DO THIS....

DATE:

GRATITUDE	FOCUS
1.	
2.	
3.	

HEADSPACE

HEARTSPACE

TODAY I AM CHOOSING TO BELIEVE...

TODAY I AM HONORING _____ BY:

I AM SCARED OF _____
BUT I AM GOING TO DO THIS....

September

SEPTEMBER

IN AUGUST, I WAS PROUD OF...

IN AUGUST, I WAS CHALLENGED BY...

THEME

WAYS OF BEING

THIS MONTH, HONORING MY THEME AND WAYS OF BEING MEANS...

daily prompt

WHAT'S MY PURPOSE?
HOW CAN I/DID I EXPRESS MY PURPOSE TODAY?

Your purpose may not be solidified yet, but practice working with what you've got.

By asking this daily, you'll begin to realize that you have many opportunities to express your purpose — from tiny expressions to huge choices, from your work to your play, from how you show up in your own skin to how you treat others.

Every day is a new chance to share your unique gifts + self with the world.

Take those chances, babe!

DATE:

GRATITUDE	FOCUS
1.	
2.	
3.	

HEADSPACE

HEARTSPACE

TODAY I AM CHOOSING TO BELIEVE...

TODAY I AM HONORING _____ BY:

WHAT'S MY PURPOSE? HOW CAN I/DID I EXPRESS MY PURPOSE TODAY?

DATE:

GRATITUDE	FOCUS
1.	
2.	
3.	

HEADSPACE

HEARTSPACE

TODAY I AM CHOOSING TO BELIEVE...

TODAY I AM HONORING _____ BY:

WHAT'S MY PURPOSE? HOW CAN I/DID I EXPRESS MY PURPOSE TODAY?

DATE:

GRATITUDE	FOCUS
1.	
2.	
3.	

HEADSPACE

HEARTSPACE

TODAY I AM CHOOSING TO BELIEVE...

TODAY I AM HONORING _____ BY:

WHAT'S MY PURPOSE? HOW CAN I/DID I EXPRESS MY PURPOSE TODAY?

DATE:

GRATITUDE	FOCUS
1.	
2.	
3.	

HEADSPACE

HEARTSPACE

TODAY I AM CHOOSING TO BELIEVE...

TODAY I AM HONORING _____ BY:

WHAT'S MY PURPOSE? HOW CAN I/DID I EXPRESS MY PURPOSE TODAY?

DATE:

GRATITUDE	FOCUS
1.	
2.	
3.	

HEADSPACE

HEARTSPACE

TODAY I AM CHOOSING TO BELIEVE...

TODAY I AM HONORING _____ BY:

WHAT'S MY PURPOSE? HOW CAN I/DID I EXPRESS MY PURPOSE TODAY?

DATE:

GRATITUDE	FOCUS
1.	
2.	
3.	

HEADSPACE | | | **HEARTSPACE**

TODAY I AM CHOOSING TO BELIEVE...

TODAY I AM HONORING _____ BY:

WHAT'S MY PURPOSE? HOW CAN I/DID I EXPRESS MY PURPOSE TODAY?

DATE:

GRATITUDE	FOCUS
1.	
2.	
3.	

HEADSPACE

HEARTSPACE

TODAY I AM CHOOSING TO BELIEVE...

TODAY I AM HONORING _____ BY:

WHAT'S MY PURPOSE? HOW CAN I/DID I EXPRESS MY PURPOSE TODAY?

DATE:

GRATITUDE	FOCUS
1.	
2.	
3.	

HEADSPACE

HEARTSPACE

TODAY I AM CHOOSING TO BELIEVE...

TODAY I AM HONORING _____ BY:

WHAT'S MY PURPOSE? HOW CAN I/DID I EXPRESS MY PURPOSE TODAY?

DATE:

GRATITUDE	FOCUS
1.	
2.	
3.	

HEADSPACE			HEARTSPACE

TODAY I AM CHOOSING TO BELIEVE...

TODAY I AM HONORING _____ BY:

WHAT'S MY PURPOSE? HOW CAN I/DID I EXPRESS MY PURPOSE TODAY?

DATE:

GRATITUDE	FOCUS
1.	
2.	
3.	

HEADSPACE			HEARTSPACE

TODAY I AM CHOOSING TO BELIEVE...

TODAY I AM HONORING _____ BY:

WHAT'S MY PURPOSE? HOW CAN I/DID I EXPRESS MY PURPOSE TODAY?

DATE:

GRATITUDE	FOCUS
1.	
2.	
3.	

HEADSPACE

HEARTSPACE

TODAY I AM CHOOSING TO BELIEVE...

TODAY I AM HONORING _____ BY:

WHAT'S MY PURPOSE? HOW CAN I/DID I EXPRESS MY PURPOSE TODAY?

DATE:

GRATITUDE	FOCUS
1.	
2.	
3.	

HEADSPACE

HEARTSPACE

TODAY I AM CHOOSING TO BELIEVE...

TODAY I AM HONORING _____ BY:

WHAT'S MY PURPOSE? HOW CAN I/DID I EXPRESS MY PURPOSE TODAY?

DATE:

GRATITUDE	FOCUS
1.	
2.	
3.	

HEADSPACE

HEARTSPACE

TODAY I AM CHOOSING TO BELIEVE...

TODAY I AM HONORING _____ BY:

WHAT'S MY PURPOSE? HOW CAN I/DID I EXPRESS MY PURPOSE TODAY?

DATE:

GRATITUDE	FOCUS
1.	
2.	
3.	

	HEADSPACE			HEARTSPACE

TODAY I AM CHOOSING TO BELIEVE...

TODAY I AM HONORING _____ BY:

WHAT'S MY PURPOSE? HOW CAN I/DID I EXPRESS MY PURPOSE TODAY?

DATE:

GRATITUDE	FOCUS
1.	
2.	
3.	

HEADSPACE

HEARTSPACE

TODAY I AM CHOOSING TO BELIEVE...

TODAY I AM HONORING _____ BY:

WHAT'S MY PURPOSE? HOW CAN I/DID I EXPRESS MY PURPOSE TODAY?

DATE:

GRATITUDE	FOCUS
1.	
2.	
3.	

HEADSPACE

HEARTSPACE

TODAY I AM CHOOSING TO BELIEVE...

TODAY I AM HONORING _____ BY:

WHAT'S MY PURPOSE? HOW CAN I/DID I EXPRESS MY PURPOSE TODAY?

DATE:

GRATITUDE	FOCUS
1.	
2.	
3.	

HEADSPACE

HEARTSPACE

TODAY I AM CHOOSING TO BELIEVE...

TODAY I AM HONORING _____ BY:

WHAT'S MY PURPOSE? HOW CAN I/DID I EXPRESS MY PURPOSE TODAY?

DATE:

GRATITUDE	FOCUS
1.	
2.	
3.	

HEADSPACE

HEARTSPACE

TODAY I AM CHOOSING TO BELIEVE...

TODAY I AM HONORING _____ BY:

WHAT'S MY PURPOSE? HOW CAN I/DID I EXPRESS MY PURPOSE TODAY?

DATE:

GRATITUDE	FOCUS
1.	
2.	
3.	

HEADSPACE

HEARTSPACE

TODAY I AM CHOOSING TO BELIEVE...

TODAY I AM HONORING _____ BY:

WHAT'S MY PURPOSE? HOW CAN I/DID I EXPRESS MY PURPOSE TODAY?

DATE:

GRATITUDE	FOCUS
1.	
2.	
3.	

HEADSPACE

HEARTSPACE

TODAY I AM CHOOSING TO BELIEVE...

TODAY I AM HONORING _____ BY:

WHAT'S MY PURPOSE? HOW CAN I/DID I EXPRESS MY PURPOSE TODAY?

October

OCTOBER

IN SEPTEMBER, I WAS PROUD OF...

IN SEPTEMBER, I WAS CHALLENGED BY...

THEME

WAYS OF BEING

THIS MONTH, HONORING MY THEME AND WAYS OF BEING MEANS...

daily prompt

WHERE AM I EXPRESSING MY TRUTH?
WHERE DO I FEEL SILENCED?

To be powerful, you must be both self-aware enough to know what your truth is and also, strong enough to stand up for that truth in the world.

This month's prompt is simply about being in tune with how you are both using and giving away your own power on a daily basis.

When you know better, you do better...

DATE:

GRATITUDE	FOCUS
1.	
2.	
3.	

HEADSPACE			HEARTSPACE

TODAY I AM CHOOSING TO BELIEVE...

TODAY I AM HONORING _____ BY:

WHERE AM I EXPRESSING MY TRUTH?

WHERE DO I FEEL SILENCED?

DATE:

GRATITUDE	FOCUS
1.	
2.	
3.	

HEADSPACE

HEARTSPACE

TODAY I AM CHOOSING TO BELIEVE...

TODAY I AM HONORING _____ BY:

WHERE AM I EXPRESSING MY TRUTH?

WHERE DO I FEEL SILENCED?

DATE:

GRATITUDE	FOCUS
1.	
2.	
3.	

HEADSPACE			HEARTSPACE

TODAY I AM CHOOSING TO BELIEVE...

TODAY I AM HONORING _____ BY:

WHERE AM I EXPRESSING MY TRUTH?

WHERE DO I FEEL SILENCED?

DATE:

GRATITUDE	FOCUS
1.	
2.	
3.	

HEADSPACE

HEARTSPACE

TODAY I AM CHOOSING TO BELIEVE...

TODAY I AM HONORING _____ BY:

WHERE AM I EXPRESSING MY TRUTH?

WHERE DO I FEEL SILENCED?

DATE:

GRATITUDE	FOCUS
1.	
2.	
3.	

HEADSPACE

HEARTSPACE

TODAY I AM CHOOSING TO BELIEVE...

TODAY I AM HONORING _____ BY:

WHERE AM I EXPRESSING MY TRUTH?

WHERE DO I FEEL SILENCED?

DATE:

GRATITUDE	FOCUS
1.	
2.	
3.	

HEADSPACE

HEARTSPACE

TODAY I AM CHOOSING TO BELIEVE...

TODAY I AM HONORING _____ BY:

WHERE AM I EXPRESSING MY TRUTH?

WHERE DO I FEEL SILENCED?

DATE:

GRATITUDE	FOCUS
1.	
2.	
3.	

HEADSPACE

HEARTSPACE

TODAY I AM CHOOSING TO BELIEVE...

TODAY I AM HONORING _____ BY:

WHERE AM I EXPRESSING MY TRUTH?

WHERE DO I FEEL SILENCED?

DATE:

GRATITUDE	FOCUS
1.	
2.	
3.	

HEADSPACE | | **HEARTSPACE**

TODAY I AM CHOOSING TO BELIEVE...

TODAY I AM HONORING _____ BY:

WHERE AM I EXPRESSING MY TRUTH?

WHERE DO I FEEL SILENCED?

DATE:

GRATITUDE	FOCUS
1.	
2.	
3.	

HEADSPACE

HEARTSPACE

TODAY I AM CHOOSING TO BELIEVE...

TODAY I AM HONORING _____ BY:

WHERE AM I EXPRESSING MY TRUTH?

WHERE DO I FEEL SILENCED?

DATE:

GRATITUDE	FOCUS
1.	
2.	
3.	

HEADSPACE

HEARTSPACE

TODAY I AM CHOOSING TO BELIEVE...

TODAY I AM HONORING _____ BY:

WHERE AM I EXPRESSING MY TRUTH?

WHERE DO I FEEL SILENCED?

DATE:

GRATITUDE	FOCUS
1.	
2.	
3.	

HEADSPACE

HEARTSPACE

TODAY I AM CHOOSING TO BELIEVE...

TODAY I AM HONORING _____ BY:

WHERE AM I EXPRESSING MY TRUTH?

WHERE DO I FEEL SILENCED?

DATE:

GRATITUDE	FOCUS
1.	
2.	
3.	

HEADSPACE

HEARTSPACE

TODAY I AM CHOOSING TO BELIEVE...

TODAY I AM HONORING _____ BY:

WHERE AM I EXPRESSING MY TRUTH?

WHERE DO I FEEL SILENCED?

DATE:

GRATITUDE	FOCUS
1.	
2.	
3.	

HEADSPACE

HEARTSPACE

TODAY I AM CHOOSING TO BELIEVE...

TODAY I AM HONORING _____ BY:

WHERE AM I EXPRESSING MY TRUTH?

WHERE DO I FEEL SILENCED?

DATE:

GRATITUDE	FOCUS
1.	
2.	
3.	

HEADSPACE

HEARTSPACE

TODAY I AM CHOOSING TO BELIEVE...

TODAY I AM HONORING _____ BY:

WHERE AM I EXPRESSING MY TRUTH?

WHERE DO I FEEL SILENCED?

DATE:

GRATITUDE	FOCUS
1.	
2.	
3.	

HEADSPACE

HEARTSPACE

TODAY I AM CHOOSING TO BELIEVE...

TODAY I AM HONORING _____ BY:

WHERE AM I EXPRESSING MY TRUTH?

WHERE DO I FEEL SILENCED?

DATE:

GRATITUDE	FOCUS
1.	
2.	
3.	

HEADSPACE

HEARTSPACE

TODAY I AM CHOOSING TO BELIEVE...

TODAY I AM HONORING _____ BY:

WHERE AM I EXPRESSING MY TRUTH?

WHERE DO I FEEL SILENCED?

DATE:

GRATITUDE	FOCUS
1.	
2.	
3.	

HEADSPACE

HEARTSPACE

TODAY I AM CHOOSING TO BELIEVE...

TODAY I AM HONORING _____ BY:

WHERE AM I EXPRESSING MY TRUTH?

WHERE DO I FEEL SILENCED?

DATE:

GRATITUDE	FOCUS
1.	
2.	
3.	

HEADSPACE

HEARTSPACE

TODAY I AM CHOOSING TO BELIEVE...

TODAY I AM HONORING _____ BY:

WHERE AM I EXPRESSING MY TRUTH?

WHERE DO I FEEL SILENCED?

DATE:

GRATITUDE	FOCUS
1.	
2.	
3.	

HEADSPACE

HEARTSPACE

TODAY I AM CHOOSING TO BELIEVE...

TODAY I AM HONORING _____ BY:

WHERE AM I EXPRESSING MY TRUTH?

WHERE DO I FEEL SILENCED?

DATE:

GRATITUDE	FOCUS
1.	
2.	
3.	

HEADSPACE | | | **HEARTSPACE**

TODAY I AM CHOOSING TO BELIEVE...

TODAY I AM HONORING _____ BY:

WHERE AM I EXPRESSING MY TRUTH?

WHERE DO I FEEL SILENCED?

November

NOVEMBER

IN OCTOBER, I WAS PROUD OF...

IN OCTOBER, I WAS CHALLENGED BY...

THEME

WAYS OF BEING

THIS MONTH, HONORING MY THEME AND WAYS OF BEING MEANS...

daily prompt

3 WAYS I AM ABUNDANT?

Financial, personal, spiritual, social, physical, professional — what are all the ways you are blessed with abundance, with plenty, with enough?

The more you recognize and celebrate your current state of sufficiency — the more you will be rewarded.

Use this daily prompt to practice gratitude for all you have.

NOVEMBER

IN OCTOBER, I WAS PROUD OF...

IN OCTOBER, I WAS CHALLENGED BY...

THEME

WAYS OF BEING

THIS MONTH, HONORING MY THEME AND WAYS OF BEING MEANS...

DATE:

GRATITUDE	FOCUS
1.	
2.	
3.	

HEADSPACE | | **HEARTSPACE**

TODAY I AM CHOOSING TO BELIEVE...

TODAY I AM HONORING _____ BY:

3 WAYS I AM ABUNDANT?

1.

2.

3.

DATE:

GRATITUDE	FOCUS
1.	
2.	
3.	

HEADSPACE

HEARTSPACE

TODAY I AM CHOOSING TO BELIEVE...

TODAY I AM HONORING _____ BY:

3 WAYS I AM ABUNDANT?

1.

2.

3.

DATE:

GRATITUDE	FOCUS
1.	
2.	
3.	

HEADSPACE | | | **HEARTSPACE**

TODAY I AM CHOOSING TO BELIEVE...

TODAY I AM HONORING _____ BY:

3 WAYS I AM ABUNDANT?

1.

2.

3.

DATE:

GRATITUDE	FOCUS
1.	
2.	
3.	

HEADSPACE

HEARTSPACE

TODAY I AM CHOOSING TO BELIEVE...

TODAY I AM HONORING _____ BY:

3 WAYS I AM ABUNDANT?

1.

2.

3.

DATE:

GRATITUDE	FOCUS
1.	
2.	
3.	

HEADSPACE | | | **HEARTSPACE**

TODAY I AM CHOOSING TO BELIEVE...

TODAY I AM HONORING _____ BY:

3 WAYS I AM ABUNDANT?

1.

2.

3.

DATE:

GRATITUDE	FOCUS
1.	
2.	
3.	

HEADSPACE

HEARTSPACE

TODAY I AM CHOOSING TO BELIEVE...

TODAY I AM HONORING _____ BY:

3 WAYS I AM ABUNDANT?

1.

2.

3.

DATE:

GRATITUDE	FOCUS
1.	
2.	
3.	

HEADSPACE

HEARTSPACE

TODAY I AM CHOOSING TO BELIEVE...

TODAY I AM HONORING _____ BY:

3 WAYS I AM ABUNDANT?

1.

2.

3.

DATE:

GRATITUDE	FOCUS
1.	
2.	
3.	

HEADSPACE

HEARTSPACE

TODAY I AM CHOOSING TO BELIEVE...

TODAY I AM HONORING _____ BY:

3 WAYS I AM ABUNDANT?

1.

2.

3.

DATE:

GRATITUDE	FOCUS
1.	
2.	
3.	

HEADSPACE

HEARTSPACE

TODAY I AM CHOOSING TO BELIEVE...

TODAY I AM HONORING _____ BY:

3 WAYS I AM ABUNDANT?

1.

2.

3.

DATE:

GRATITUDE	FOCUS
1.	
2.	
3.	

HEADSPACE

HEARTSPACE

TODAY I AM CHOOSING TO BELIEVE...

TODAY I AM HONORING _____ BY:

3 WAYS I AM ABUNDANT?

1.

2.

3.

DATE:

GRATITUDE	FOCUS
1.	
2.	
3.	

HEADSPACE

HEARTSPACE

TODAY I AM CHOOSING TO BELIEVE...

TODAY I AM HONORING _____ BY:

3 WAYS I AM ABUNDANT?

1.

2.

3.

DATE:

GRATITUDE	FOCUS
1.	
2.	
3.	

HEADSPACE

HEARTSPACE

TODAY I AM CHOOSING TO BELIEVE...

TODAY I AM HONORING _____ BY:

3 WAYS I AM ABUNDANT?

1.

2.

3.

DATE:

GRATITUDE	FOCUS
1.	
2.	
3.	

HEADSPACE

HEARTSPACE

TODAY I AM CHOOSING TO BELIEVE...

TODAY I AM HONORING _____ BY:

3 WAYS I AM ABUNDANT?

1.

2.

3.

DATE:

GRATITUDE	FOCUS
1.	
2.	
3.	

HEADSPACE

HEARTSPACE

TODAY I AM CHOOSING TO BELIEVE...

TODAY I AM HONORING _____ BY:

3 WAYS I AM ABUNDANT?

1.

2.

3.

DATE:

GRATITUDE	FOCUS
1.	
2.	
3.	

<table>
<tr><td>HEADSPACE</td><td></td><td></td><td>HEARTSPACE</td></tr>
</table>

TODAY I AM CHOOSING TO BELIEVE...

TODAY I AM HONORING _____ BY:

3 WAYS I AM ABUNDANT?

1.

2.

3.

DATE:

GRATITUDE	FOCUS
1.	
2.	
3.	

HEADSPACE

HEARTSPACE

TODAY I AM CHOOSING TO BELIEVE...

TODAY I AM HONORING _____ BY:

3 WAYS I AM ABUNDANT?

1.

2.

3.

DATE:

GRATITUDE	FOCUS
1.	
2.	
3.	

HEADSPACE

HEARTSPACE

TODAY I AM CHOOSING TO BELIEVE...

TODAY I AM HONORING _____ BY:

3 WAYS I AM ABUNDANT?

1.

2.

3.

DATE:

GRATITUDE	FOCUS
1.	
2.	
3.	

HEADSPACE

HEARTSPACE

TODAY I AM CHOOSING TO BELIEVE...

TODAY I AM HONORING _____ BY:

3 WAYS I AM ABUNDANT?

1.

2.

3.

DATE:

GRATITUDE	FOCUS
1.	
2.	
3.	

HEADSPACE

HEARTSPACE

TODAY I AM CHOOSING TO BELIEVE...

TODAY I AM HONORING _____ BY:

3 WAYS I AM ABUNDANT?

1.

2.

3.

DATE:

GRATITUDE	FOCUS
1.	
2.	
3.	

HEADSPACE

HEARTSPACE

TODAY I AM CHOOSING TO BELIEVE...

TODAY I AM HONORING _____ BY:

3 WAYS I AM ABUNDANT?

1.

2.

3.

DATE:

GRATITUDE	FOCUS
1.	
2.	
3.	

HEADSPACE

HEARTSPACE

TODAY I AM CHOOSING TO BELIEVE...

TODAY I AM HONORING _____ BY:

3 WAYS I AM ABUNDANT?

1.

2.

3.

December

DECEMBER

IN NOVEMBER, I WAS PROUD OF...

IN NOVEMBER, I WAS CHALLENGED BY...

THEME

WAYS OF BEING

THIS MONTH, HONORING MY THEME AND WAYS OF BEING MEANS...

daily prompt

WHAT DO I WANT TO REMEMBER ABOUT THIS YEAR?

You're heavy into a month of reflection, so use this prompt to gather all the beauty, the lessons or the tiny moments that you want to remember about this year.

It can be a treasured memory, a belief that finally took hold, a lightening strike of inspiration, an inkling of desire, or an event that rocked you.

Savor the small snapshots that make up your life, honey.

DATE:

GRATITUDE	FOCUS
1.	
2.	
3.	

HEADSPACE

HEARTSPACE

TODAY I AM CHOOSING TO BELIEVE...

TODAY I AM HONORING _____ BY:

WHAT DO I WANT TO REMEMBER ABOUT THIS YEAR?

1.

2.

3.

DATE:

GRATITUDE	FOCUS
1.	
2.	
3.	

HEADSPACE

HEARTSPACE

TODAY I AM CHOOSING TO BELIEVE...

TODAY I AM HONORING _____ BY:

WHAT DO I WANT TO REMEMBER ABOUT THIS YEAR?

1.

2.

3.

DATE:

GRATITUDE	FOCUS
1.	
2.	
3.	

HEADSPACE

HEARTSPACE

TODAY I AM CHOOSING TO BELIEVE...

TODAY I AM HONORING _____ BY:

WHAT DO I WANT TO REMEMBER ABOUT THIS YEAR?

1.

2.

3.

DATE:

GRATITUDE	FOCUS
1.	
2.	
3.	

HEADSPACE

HEARTSPACE

TODAY I AM CHOOSING TO BELIEVE...

TODAY I AM HONORING _____ BY:

WHAT DO I WANT TO REMEMBER ABOUT THIS YEAR?

1.

2.

3.

DATE:

GRATITUDE	FOCUS
1.	
2.	
3.	

HEADSPACE

HEARTSPACE

TODAY I AM CHOOSING TO BELIEVE...

TODAY I AM HONORING _____ BY:

WHAT DO I WANT TO REMEMBER ABOUT THIS YEAR?

1.

2.

3.

DATE:

GRATITUDE	**FOCUS**
1.	
2.	
3.	

HEADSPACE

HEARTSPACE

TODAY I AM CHOOSING TO BELIEVE...

TODAY I AM HONORING _____ BY:

WHAT DO I WANT TO REMEMBER ABOUT THIS YEAR?

1.

2.

3.

DATE:

GRATITUDE	FOCUS
1.	
2.	
3.	

HEADSPACE

HEARTSPACE

TODAY I AM CHOOSING TO BELIEVE...

TODAY I AM HONORING _____ BY:

WHAT DO I WANT TO REMEMBER ABOUT THIS YEAR?

1.

2.

3.

DATE:

GRATITUDE	FOCUS
1.	
2.	
3.	

HEADSPACE

HEARTSPACE

TODAY I AM CHOOSING TO BELIEVE...

TODAY I AM HONORING _____ BY:

WHAT DO I WANT TO REMEMBER ABOUT THIS YEAR?

1.

2.

3.

DATE:

GRATITUDE	FOCUS
1.	
2.	
3.	

HEADSPACE

HEARTSPACE

TODAY I AM CHOOSING TO BELIEVE...

TODAY I AM HONORING _____ BY:

WHAT DO I WANT TO REMEMBER ABOUT THIS YEAR?

1.

2.

3.

DATE:

GRATITUDE	FOCUS
1.	
2.	
3.	

HEADSPACE

HEARTSPACE

TODAY I AM CHOOSING TO BELIEVE...

TODAY I AM HONORING _____ BY:

WHAT DO I WANT TO REMEMBER ABOUT THIS YEAR?

1.

2.

3.

DATE:

GRATITUDE	FOCUS
1.	
2.	
3.	

HEADSPACE

HEARTSPACE

TODAY I AM CHOOSING TO BELIEVE...

TODAY I AM HONORING _____ BY:

WHAT DO I WANT TO REMEMBER ABOUT THIS YEAR?

1.

2.

3.

DATE:

GRATITUDE	FOCUS
1.	
2.	
3.	

HEADSPACE

HEARTSPACE

TODAY I AM CHOOSING TO BELIEVE...

TODAY I AM HONORING _____ BY:

WHAT DO I WANT TO REMEMBER ABOUT THIS YEAR?

1.

2.

3.

DATE:

GRATITUDE	FOCUS
1.	
2.	
3.	

HEADSPACE

HEARTSPACE

TODAY I AM CHOOSING TO BELIEVE...

TODAY I AM HONORING _____ BY:

WHAT DO I WANT TO REMEMBER ABOUT THIS YEAR?

1.

2.

3.

DATE:

GRATITUDE	FOCUS
1.	
2.	
3.	

HEADSPACE | | **HEARTSPACE**

TODAY I AM CHOOSING TO BELIEVE...

TODAY I AM HONORING _____ BY:

WHAT DO I WANT TO REMEMBER ABOUT THIS YEAR?

1.

2.

3.

DATE:

GRATITUDE	FOCUS
1.	
2.	
3.	

HEADSPACE

HEARTSPACE

TODAY I AM CHOOSING TO BELIEVE...

TODAY I AM HONORING _____ BY:

WHAT DO I WANT TO REMEMBER ABOUT THIS YEAR?

1.

2.

3.

DATE:

GRATITUDE	FOCUS
1.	
2.	
3.	

HEADSPACE

HEARTSPACE

TODAY I AM CHOOSING TO BELIEVE...

TODAY I AM HONORING _____ BY:

WHAT DO I WANT TO REMEMBER ABOUT THIS YEAR?

1.

2.

3.

DATE:

GRATITUDE	FOCUS
1.	
2.	
3.	

HEADSPACE

HEARTSPACE

TODAY I AM CHOOSING TO BELIEVE...

TODAY I AM HONORING _____ BY:

WHAT DO I WANT TO REMEMBER ABOUT THIS YEAR?

1.

2.

3.

DATE:

GRATITUDE	FOCUS
1.	
2.	
3.	

HEADSPACE

HEARTSPACE

TODAY I AM CHOOSING TO BELIEVE...

TODAY I AM HONORING _____ BY:

WHAT DO I WANT TO REMEMBER ABOUT THIS YEAR?

1.

2.

3.

DATE:

GRATITUDE	FOCUS
1.	
2.	
3.	

HEADSPACE

HEARTSPACE

TODAY I AM CHOOSING TO BELIEVE...

TODAY I AM HONORING _____ BY:

WHAT DO I WANT TO REMEMBER ABOUT THIS YEAR?

1.

2.

3.

DATE:

GRATITUDE	FOCUS
1.	
2.	
3.	

HEADSPACE

HEARTSPACE

TODAY I AM CHOOSING TO BELIEVE...

TODAY I AM HONORING _____ BY:

WHAT DO I WANT TO REMEMBER ABOUT THIS YEAR?

1.

2.

3.

Made in the USA
Las Vegas, NV
13 October 2021

32252117R00176